Microsoft PowerPoint

The Microsoft 365 Companion Series

Dr. Patrick Jones

OLYMPUS ACADEMY
PRESS

Copyright © 2024 by Patrick Jones

All rights reserved, including the right to reproduce this book or portions thereof in any form.

TABLE OF CONTENTS

Elevating Your Presentations 1
What Is Microsoft PowerPoint? 5
Why Use Microsoft PowerPoint? 9
Getting Started with Microsoft PowerPoint 15
Best Practices for Microsoft PowerPoint 21
Tips and Tricks for Microsoft PowerPoint 27
Your AI-Powered Presentation Partner 33
Common Pitfalls and How to Avoid Them 37
Sarah's PowerPoint Transformation 43
Lessons from PowerPoint and Sarah's Journey 47
PowerPoint and Beyond 51

ELEVATING YOUR PRESENTATIONS

Imagine standing before an audience, whether in a boardroom, classroom, or virtual meeting, armed with a presentation that not only informs but captivates. That's the magic of Microsoft PowerPoint—a tool that transforms ideas into impactful visuals, elevating your communication and leaving a lasting impression.

For decades, PowerPoint has been synonymous with presentations, and for good reason. It's a versatile platform that empowers users to create everything from simple slide decks to dynamic, multimedia-rich presentations. But PowerPoint is much more than just slides—it's a canvas for creativity, a storytelling tool, and a bridge between your message and your audience.

In this book, we'll explore the full potential of Microsoft PowerPoint, breaking down its features and functionalities in a way that's approachable, educational, and inspiring. Whether you're new to PowerPoint or looking to refine your skills, this guide will equip you with the knowledge and confidence to create presentations that stand out.

In a world where communication is more visual than ever, PowerPoint remains a cornerstone of professional and educational environments. Its value lies in its adaptability:

- **For Professionals:** Craft compelling pitches, share data insights, and lead impactful meetings.
- **For Educators:** Design engaging lessons, simplify complex topics, and foster interactive learning.
- **For Everyone Else:** Create memorable presentations for events, personal projects, or community initiatives.

PowerPoint's relevance has only grown with its integration into Microsoft 365, allowing for seamless collaboration, cloud-based access, and innovative features like AI-powered design assistance.

This book is your comprehensive guide to mastering PowerPoint, from the basics to advanced tips and tricks. Here's a sneak peek at what's ahead:

- **What Is PowerPoint?** A foundational look at PowerPoint's capabilities and its place within the Microsoft 365 suite.
- **Why Use PowerPoint?** Discover the unique benefits of PowerPoint and how it can elevate your storytelling.
- **Getting Started:** Step-by-step guidance on creating your first presentation, from choosing templates to adding slides.
- **Best Practices:** Learn design principles and techniques to make your presentations visually stunning and effective.
- **Tips and Tricks:** Uncover hidden features and shortcuts to save time and enhance your workflow.
- **Copilot for PowerPoint:** Harness AI-powered tools to create smarter, more polished presentations.
- **Common Pitfalls:** Avoid common mistakes that can detract from your message and impact.
- **Sarah's Journey:** Follow a relatable story of growth and learning as Sarah masters PowerPoint for her team's big presentation.
- **Summary and Reflection:** Recap key lessons and see how Sarah's story parallels your journey.
- **Final Thoughts:** Explore how PowerPoint fits into the larger Microsoft 365 ecosystem and discover resources for continued learning.

As with the other books in the *Microsoft 365 Companion Series*, we'll follow Sarah—a professional navigating the challenges of modern work—as she learns to harness the power of PowerPoint. Her relatable journey will show you how to overcome obstacles, unlock creativity, and achieve success.

Whether you're creating your first slide deck or refining an important presentation, this book is designed to make PowerPoint accessible and enjoyable. Written in a conversational style, it breaks down complex topics into easy-to-understand steps, blending education with inspiration to keep you engaged.

By the time you reach the final chapter, you'll have the tools, confidence, and creativity to deliver presentations that make an impact. Let's begin this exciting journey into the world of Microsoft PowerPoint together!

WHAT IS MICROSOFT POWERPOINT?

Microsoft PowerPoint is a powerful presentation software that has become the gold standard for creating visually compelling and engaging slide decks. From its humble beginnings in the late 1980s to its current role as a cornerstone of the Microsoft 365 suite, PowerPoint has evolved to meet the diverse needs of professionals, educators, and individuals worldwide.

At its core, PowerPoint is a tool that allows users to create, customize, and deliver presentations. But it's much more than that—it's a platform for storytelling, an aid for visual communication, and a creative outlet for designing content that resonates with audiences.

PowerPoint provides a framework for creating presentations using a series of slides. Each slide acts as a blank canvas where you can add text, images, charts, videos, and animations to convey your message. The software offers a rich set of tools to help you design, organize, and present your ideas effectively.

Key Features Include:

- **Slide Layouts:** Pre-designed structures to arrange content.
- **Themes and Templates:** Ready-to-use designs that give your presentation a polished look.
- **Animations and Transitions:** Visual effects to make your slides dynamic.
- **Multimedia Integration:** Embed videos, audio, and images directly into your presentation.
- **Collaboration Tools:** Real-time editing and commenting through Microsoft 365.

Example: Imagine a sales team using PowerPoint to pitch a new product. They combine compelling visuals, animations, and data charts to tell a story that engages their audience and closes the deal.

In today's world, where attention spans are short, and information overload is common, PowerPoint plays a critical role in simplifying complex ideas and making them memorable.

- **For Businesses:** PowerPoint is a go-to tool for crafting sales pitches, presenting financial reports, and sharing project updates.
- **For Educators:** Teachers use PowerPoint to create visually engaging lessons that keep students focused and enhance learning.
- **For Individuals:** From personal projects to community presentations, PowerPoint empowers users to express themselves creatively.

Pro Tip: Use PowerPoint's built-in design tools, like the Designer feature, to create professional-looking slides with minimal effort.

One of PowerPoint's greatest strengths is its seamless integration with Microsoft 365. This integration opens up a world of possibilities for collaboration, accessibility, and efficiency.

- **Collaboration:** Work on presentations with your team in real-time, whether you're in the same office or across the globe.
- **Cloud Access:** Save your presentations to OneDrive or SharePoint for easy access from any device.
- **Integration with Teams:** Present directly in Teams meetings with a single click.
- **Data Integration:** Import data from Excel to create dynamic charts and graphs.

Example: Sarah, preparing for her company's annual meeting, collaborated with her team using PowerPoint in Microsoft Teams. Each team member contributed slides in real-time, ensuring the presentation was ready ahead of schedule.

Over the years, PowerPoint has introduced features that keep it ahead of the curve, such as:

- **AI-Powered Design Suggestions:** The Designer tool suggests layouts and visuals to enhance your slides.
- **Presenter Coach:** Practice your delivery with real-time feedback on pacing, filler words, and tone.
- **Interactive Features:** Add quizzes, polls, and live Q&A to engage your audience.

Pro Tip: Use the Presenter Coach feature to rehearse and refine your presentation skills before the big day.

While PowerPoint is incredibly versatile, it's often misunderstood or misused. Some may think it's outdated or only suitable for traditional presentations, but the truth is, PowerPoint is a creative powerhouse when used to its full potential.

Misconception 1: "PowerPoint is boring."
Reality: With tools like animations, multimedia integration, and AI design, PowerPoint can be as dynamic and engaging as you make it.

Misconception 2: "PowerPoint is hard to use."
Reality: PowerPoint's user-friendly interface and pre-designed templates make it accessible to beginners while offering advanced tools for power users.

Example: Sarah initially thought PowerPoint was just for slides. After exploring its features, she realized she could create animated videos, interactive quizzes, and even infographics—all within PowerPoint.

What sets PowerPoint apart from other presentation tools is its combination of simplicity and depth. Beginners can create a basic slide deck in minutes, while advanced users can produce complex, multimedia-rich presentations.

Standout Features Include:

- **Flexibility:** Suitable for a wide range of uses, from professional pitches to educational lessons.
- **Customization:** Personalize every element of your slides, from fonts and colors to animations and transitions.
- **Integration:** Work seamlessly with other Microsoft 365 tools for a unified experience.

Now that you understand what PowerPoint is and its role in modern communication, it's time to explore why this tool is indispensable for professionals, educators, and individuals alike.

WHY USE MICROSOFT POWERPOINT?

Microsoft PowerPoint is more than a tool for creating slide decks—it's a platform for transforming ideas into engaging, visually compelling narratives. Whether you're presenting to a packed conference room, leading a virtual meeting, or sharing a quick update with your team, PowerPoint empowers you to communicate with clarity, creativity, and impact.

In this chapter, we'll explore the unique benefits of PowerPoint, diving into why it remains the go-to presentation tool for professionals, educators, and individuals around the world.

1. Turn Complex Ideas into Visual Narratives

Why It Matters:
A picture is worth a thousand words, and PowerPoint excels at turning complex data and concepts into visuals that are easy to understand.

How It Helps:

- Create charts, graphs, and infographics to present data visually.
- Use SmartArt to simplify processes, hierarchies, or workflows.
- Leverage multimedia elements like videos and animations to tell a compelling story.

Example: Sarah used PowerPoint to transform a dense financial report into an engaging presentation with colorful charts and animations, making it accessible to her non-financial audience.

Pro Tip: Use PowerPoint's Designer feature to automatically suggest layouts and designs that enhance your slides.

2. Enhance Audience Engagement

Why It Matters:
Keeping your audience's attention is critical, and PowerPoint offers tools to make your presentations dynamic and interactive.

How It Helps:

- Use animations and transitions to highlight key points.
- Add interactive elements like clickable links or embedded polls.
- Enable real-time Q&A sessions through PowerPoint Live in Teams.

Example: During a virtual training session, Sarah embedded a live quiz into her PowerPoint slides, keeping participants engaged and reinforcing learning.

Pro Tip: Balance animations and transitions—use them to emphasize key points without overwhelming your audience.

3. Seamless Integration with Microsoft 365

Why It Matters:
PowerPoint isn't just a standalone tool—it's part of the Microsoft 365 ecosystem, making it easy to collaborate and integrate with other apps.

How It Helps:

- Save presentations to OneDrive or SharePoint for cloud access.
- Collaborate with team members in real-time using Teams.
- Embed data from Excel or videos from Stream directly into your slides.

Example: Sarah worked with her marketing team to create a product launch deck in PowerPoint. Using real-time editing in Teams, they completed the presentation together without endless email threads or version control issues.

Pro Tip: Use the Present in Teams feature to share slides directly from PowerPoint into a Teams meeting with minimal setup.

4. Accessibility and Inclusivity

Why It Matters:
Making your presentations accessible ensures everyone can engage with your content, regardless of their abilities.

How It Helps:

- Use PowerPoint's accessibility checker to identify and fix potential issues.
- Add captions to embedded videos and alt text to images.
- Enable live subtitles during presentations for a global audience.

Example: Sarah presented to a diverse team with members in multiple countries. By enabling live subtitles, she ensured everyone could follow along, regardless of language or audio challenges.

Pro Tip: Use simple, high-contrast designs to make your slides readable for all audiences.

5. Boost Confidence with Presenter Tools

Why It Matters:
Delivering a presentation can be nerve-wracking, but PowerPoint's presenter tools provide the support you need to shine.

How It Helps:

- Use Presenter View to see your notes and upcoming slides while your audience sees only the current slide.
- Practice with Presenter Coach, which provides real-time feedback on pacing, tone, and filler words.
- Record your presentation to review and refine your delivery.

Example: Before her big client pitch, Sarah used Presenter Coach to rehearse her slides. The tool flagged her tendency to speak too quickly, allowing her to adjust her pacing and deliver a polished presentation.

Pro Tip: Practice switching between slides smoothly to maintain a confident flow during your presentation.

6. Flexibility for Any Setting

Why It Matters:
From in-person meetings to virtual events, PowerPoint adapts to any setting and audience size.

How It Helps:

- Use PowerPoint Live for interactive virtual presentations.
- Export slides as PDFs for easy sharing.
- Design custom templates for consistent branding in your presentations.

Example: Sarah created a branded PowerPoint template for her company's sales team, ensuring every presentation looked professional and consistent.

Pro Tip: Customize PowerPoint templates to reflect your brand's colors, fonts, and logo.

7. Creativity Meets Simplicity

Why It Matters:
PowerPoint strikes the perfect balance between powerful features and ease of use, making it accessible to beginners while offering depth for advanced users.

How It Helps:

- Use pre-designed templates for quick, professional results.

- Explore advanced features like animations, layering, and custom slide layouts.
- Experiment with PowerPoint's *Morph* transition to create visually stunning effects.

Example: Sarah used the Morph transition to create an animated product demo within her slides, impressing her audience and securing buy-in from her leadership team.

Pro Tip: Start with templates, then gradually explore customization options to unlock your creative potential.

Despite the rise of alternative presentation tools, PowerPoint remains the gold standard because of its versatility, depth, and continuous innovation. Its ability to cater to both beginners and advanced users ensures that it adapts to your needs, no matter your skill level or objective.

PowerPoint is more than just software—it's a partner in your storytelling journey. Whether you're teaching a class, pitching a product, or sharing your vision, PowerPoint provides the tools you need to make your message memorable.

Now that you understand the value PowerPoint brings to the table, it's time to dive into the practicalities of creating your first impactful presentation.

GETTING STARTED WITH MICROSOFT POWERPOINT

Starting your journey with Microsoft PowerPoint is like stepping onto a creative stage where your ideas take center stage. PowerPoint's intuitive design makes it easy to craft compelling presentations, whether you're a beginner exploring the basics or a seasoned presenter looking for a polished product.

In this chapter, we'll guide you through the essential steps to get started with PowerPoint, ensuring you feel confident and ready to bring your ideas to life.

Step 1: Accessing Microsoft PowerPoint

PowerPoint is part of the Microsoft 365 suite, making it accessible from multiple platforms.

- **Desktop Application:** Install PowerPoint on your Windows or macOS computer for full functionality.
- **Web Version:** Use PowerPoint online through your browser by visiting office.com and signing in with your Microsoft account.
- **Mobile App:** Download the PowerPoint app on your phone or tablet for creating and editing presentations on the go.

Pro Tip: For cloud-based convenience, save your presentations to OneDrive, allowing you to access and edit them from any device.

Example: Sarah used the PowerPoint web version to quickly update slides during her commute, ensuring her presentation was ready before the meeting.

Step 2: Creating Your First Presentation

PowerPoint's user-friendly interface makes starting a presentation straightforward.

1. Open PowerPoint and select New Presentation.
2. Choose a Blank Presentation or browse through pre-designed templates for a professional look.
3. Begin by adding a title slide with your presentation's name and subtitle.

Pro Tip: If you're unsure where to start, use PowerPoint's templates, which include themes, color palettes, and font pairings to ensure a cohesive design.

Example: Sarah chose a sleek, professional template for her product launch presentation, saving her time on design while maintaining a polished appearance.

Step 3: Adding and Designing Slides

Slides are the building blocks of your presentation.

- **Add Slides:** Click New Slide in the Home tab and choose a layout that suits your content.
- **Change Layouts:** Select the slide, go to the Layout menu, and choose from options like Title Slide, Two Content, or Picture with Caption.
- **Customize Design:** Adjust colors, fonts, and backgrounds through the Design tab.

Pro Tip: Use consistent layouts to maintain visual harmony across your presentation.

Example: For her team update, Sarah used the Two Content layout to compare last quarter's performance with current trends, ensuring the data was clear and easy to follow.

Step 4: Adding Content

PowerPoint supports various types of content to make your slides dynamic and informative.

- **Text:** Add titles, subtitles, and bullet points to convey your message clearly.
- **Images:** Insert photos or graphics to support your points visually.
- **Charts and Graphs:** Visualize data by clicking Insert > Chart and choosing from options like bar graphs, pie charts, or scatter plots.
- **Multimedia:** Embed videos, audio clips, or animations to make your presentation more engaging.

Pro Tip: Keep text concise and let visuals do the heavy lifting to avoid overwhelming your audience.

Example: Sarah added a video of her product in action to a slide, allowing her audience to see its features in a real-world context.

Step 5: Customizing Your Presentation

Make your presentation uniquely yours by tailoring its design and flow.

- **Themes and Variants:** Choose a theme from the Design tab and experiment with color variants to suit your brand or topic.
- **Transitions and Animations:** Add transitions between slides or animations to individual elements for a dynamic effect.
- **Slide Order:** Rearrange slides by dragging them in the slide sorter view.

Pro Tip: Use animations sparingly to enhance, not distract from, your content.

Example: Sarah used subtle fade transitions between slides to maintain a professional tone during her investor pitch.

Step 6: Previewing and Rehearsing

Before presenting, ensure everything is in place by previewing your slides and practicing your delivery.

- **Slide Show View:** Click Slide Show to see your presentation as your audience will.
- **Presenter View:** Use this mode to see your notes, next slide, and timer while presenting.
- **Rehearse with Presenter Coach:** Practice your delivery and get feedback on pacing, filler words, and tone.

Pro Tip: Record your rehearsal to review your performance and make adjustments.

Example: Sarah rehearsed her slides using Presenter Coach, which flagged her overuse of filler words, helping her refine her delivery.

Step 7: Saving and Sharing

Once your presentation is ready, it's time to save and share it.

- **Save Locally:** Save your file as a PowerPoint presentation (.pptx) or PDF.
- **Save to the Cloud:** Store your presentation on OneDrive or SharePoint for easy access and collaboration.
- **Share:** Use the Share button to send your presentation to colleagues, or present directly in a Teams meeting.

Pro Tip: Use PowerPoint Live to present in Teams, allowing your audience to interact with your slides in real-time.

Example: Sarah saved her final presentation to OneDrive and shared the link with her team, ensuring everyone had access to the latest version.

Now that you've created your first PowerPoint presentation, you're ready to explore more advanced features and best practices.

BEST PRACTICES FOR MICROSOFT POWERPOINT

Creating a PowerPoint presentation is only half the journey; ensuring it communicates your message effectively and captivates your audience is the other half. PowerPoint offers a wealth of tools, but how you use them can make the difference between a forgettable slide deck and an impactful presentation.

In this chapter, we'll explore best practices to help you design, organize, and deliver presentations that stand out, whether you're addressing a small team or a global audience.

1. Start with a Clear Objective

Why It Matters:
Every presentation should have a purpose. Whether you're informing, persuading, or educating, clarity on your objective ensures your content aligns with your goals.

Best Practices:

- Define your key message before creating slides.
- Outline your presentation structure: Introduction, Main Content, and Conclusion.
- Tailor your content to your audience's needs and expectations.

Example: Sarah planned her product launch presentation by first identifying her key goal: convincing stakeholders to approve the new product line. She structured her slides to emphasize benefits, market opportunities, and projected ROI.

Pro Tip: Use a storytelling approach—set the stage, present the challenge, and offer a solution.

2. Keep It Simple and Focused

Why It Matters:
Overloading slides with text or visuals can confuse your audience and dilute your message. Simplicity is key to clarity.

Best Practices:

- Stick to one idea per slide.
- Use bullet points sparingly—no more than 5-6 per slide.
- Avoid clutter by balancing text, images, and white space.

Example: Sarah avoided cramming her data-heavy slides with text. Instead, she used a single graph to highlight key metrics and provided additional context verbally.

Pro Tip: Follow the 10-20-30 rule: 10 slides, 20 minutes, and 30-point font for key points.

3. Design with Visual Hierarchy in Mind

Why It Matters:
A well-designed slide guides your audience's eyes to the most important information.

Best Practices:

- Use larger fonts for titles and smaller fonts for supporting text.
- Highlight key points with bold text or contrasting colors.
- Arrange elements logically, with the most critical information at the top.

Example: In her training presentation, Sarah bolded her key takeaways and used accent colors to make them pop against a neutral background.

Pro Tip: Avoid using too many font styles or sizes—stick to 2-3 variations for consistency.

4. Choose Colors and Fonts Wisely

Why It Matters:
Colors and fonts can evoke emotions and influence readability, so choosing them carefully ensures your slides are visually appealing and professional.

Best Practices:

- Use high-contrast color combinations for readability.
- Stick to professional fonts like Arial, Calibri, or Verdana.
- Use color sparingly—accent key points, but don't overwhelm the slide.

Example: Sarah's presentation used her company's brand colors consistently, giving her slides a polished and cohesive look.

Pro Tip: Use color psychology—blue for trust, green for growth, and red for urgency—to align with your message.

5. Leverage Visuals to Enhance Understanding

Why It Matters:
Visuals can make abstract concepts tangible and data more digestible.

Best Practices:

- Use high-quality images and icons to illustrate points.
- Create charts and graphs to visualize data.
- Avoid stock photos that look overly staged or generic.

Example: Sarah used a pie chart to break down market share percentages, replacing a dense spreadsheet that would have overwhelmed her audience.

Pro Tip: Ensure all visuals align with your theme and support your message.

6. Make Animations and Transitions Subtle

Why It Matters:
Animations and transitions can add interest, but overuse can distract from your content.

Best Practices:

- Use subtle transitions like Fade or Wipe.
- Limit animations to highlighting key points or elements.
- Avoid flashy effects like Bounce or Spin unless they serve a specific purpose.

Example: Sarah used a simple Fade transition between slides and animated her sales figures to appear one by one, emphasizing their growth.

Pro Tip: Preview your animations to ensure they enhance, rather than detract from, your presentation.

7. Rehearse with Presenter Tools

Why It Matters:
Confidence comes from preparation, and PowerPoint offers tools to help you practice and refine your delivery.

Best Practices:

- Use Presenter View to see your notes, timing, and upcoming slides.
- Practice with Presenter Coach for real-time feedback on your pace and tone.
- Record a practice session to identify areas for improvement.

Example: Before her quarterly review presentation, Sarah rehearsed with Presenter Coach, which flagged her tendency to rush through key slides, allowing her to adjust her timing.

Pro Tip: Practice in the same environment where you'll present to minimize surprises.

8. Engage Your Audience

Why It Matters:
An engaged audience is more likely to remember your message and take action.

Best Practices:

- Ask questions or include interactive elements like polls or quizzes.
- Use a conversational tone and make eye contact (if presenting in person).
- Pause after key points to allow your audience to absorb the information.

Example: During her product demo, Sarah used PowerPoint Live to embed a real-time poll, gauging her audience's interest in the product's features.

Pro Tip: Use audience feedback to adapt your presentation on the fly.

9. Close with a Strong Call to Action

Why It Matters:
Your conclusion is your audience's lasting impression, so make it count.

Best Practices:

- Summarize your key points in a single slide.
- Clearly state the next steps or desired action.
- End with a memorable statement or visual.

Example: Sarah concluded her pitch with a bold slide that read, "Join Us in Shaping the Future," accompanied by a compelling product image and contact information.

Pro Tip: Practice your closing remarks to ensure they resonate with your audience.

By following these best practices, you'll elevate your PowerPoint presentations from functional to impactful.

TIPS AND TRICKS FOR MICROSOFT POWERPOINT

Microsoft PowerPoint is full of features and shortcuts that can make creating and delivering presentations easier, faster, and more impactful. These tips and tricks are designed to help you uncover hidden gems within PowerPoint, streamline your workflow, and dazzle your audience with polished, professional presentations.

1. Start with PowerPoint Designer for Instant Inspiration

The Trick:
PowerPoint's Designer tool suggests professional layouts and designs based on the content of your slides.

How to Use It:

- Add content to a slide, such as text or images.
- Open the Design Ideas pane from the Design tab.
- Select a suggested layout to apply to your slide.

Pro Tip: Use Designer to enhance your slides quickly, especially when you're short on time.

Example: Sarah added a product image to her slide, and Designer transformed it into a sleek layout with the perfect color scheme and text alignment.

2. Use Slide Master for Consistent Formatting

The Trick:
Slide Master allows you to create a consistent look across your presentation by setting global styles for fonts, colors, and layouts.

How to Use It:

- Go to the View tab and select Slide Master.
- Customize the master slide with your desired styles and branding.
- Apply the template to your presentation for consistency.

Pro Tip: Save your custom Slide Master as a template for future presentations.

Example: Sarah created a branded template for her company's sales team, ensuring every presentation followed the same professional style.

3. Use the Morph Transition for Stunning Visual Effects

The Trick:
Morph creates seamless transitions between slides, perfect for moving objects or creating animations.

How to Use It:

- Duplicate a slide and make changes to the position or size of objects.
- Apply the Morph transition to the second slide.

Pro Tip: Use Morph sparingly for impactful moments, such as revealing product features or demonstrating processes.

Example: Sarah used Morph to animate the growth of a sales chart, making her data come alive during her quarterly review.

4. Embed Multimedia for Interactive Presentations

The Trick:
Adding videos, audio clips, or interactive elements can make your presentation more engaging.

How to Use It:

- Insert videos directly from your device or link them from YouTube.

- Add audio clips for narration or background music.
- Use hyperlinks to create interactive menus or navigate between slides.

Pro Tip: Test multimedia elements before presenting to ensure they work seamlessly.

Example: Sarah embedded a product demo video into her slide, giving her audience a firsthand look at its features.

5. Add Speaker Notes for Seamless Delivery

The Trick:
Speaker notes help you stay on track during your presentation without cluttering your slides.

How to Use It:
- Add notes to the Notes pane below each slide.
- Use Presenter View to view your notes during the presentation while your audience only sees the slides.

Pro Tip: Keep your notes concise to ensure you can glance at them quickly without breaking your flow.

Example: Sarah added key talking points to her speaker notes, helping her deliver a smooth and confident pitch.

6. Use SmartArt for Visual Storytelling

The Trick:
SmartArt transforms lists and text into visually appealing graphics.

How to Use It:
- Select your text and go to Insert > SmartArt.
- Choose a layout that suits your content, such as Process, Hierarchy, or Cycle.

Pro Tip: Customize SmartArt colors and styles to match your presentation theme.

Example: Sarah converted a bulleted list of project phases into a SmartArt diagram, making her slide more engaging and professional.

7. Utilize Presenter Coach for Feedback

The Trick:
Presenter Coach offers real-time feedback on your pace, tone, and use of filler words during practice sessions.

How to Use It:

- Open your presentation in Slide Show mode.
- Select Rehearse with Coach from the options.

Pro Tip: Use Presenter Coach to refine your delivery before important meetings or events.

Example: Sarah practiced her pitch with Presenter Coach, which flagged her tendency to rush through critical slides.

8. Create Custom Animations for Impact

The Trick:
Custom animations allow you to control how objects appear, move, or exit on your slides.

How to Use It:

- Select an object and go to the Animations tab.
- Choose an animation type and customize its timing or sequence.

Pro Tip: Use animations strategically to emphasize key points rather than distracting your audience.

Example: Sarah animated her sales figures to appear one by one, keeping her audience focused on each data point as she explained it.

9. Present Like a Pro with PowerPoint Live

The Trick:
PowerPoint Live integrates seamlessly with Teams, allowing you to deliver interactive presentations and engage your audience in real-time.

How to Use It:

- Share your presentation in a Teams meeting and select PowerPoint Live.
- Allow participants to navigate slides independently if desired.

Pro Tip: Use interactive features like polls or Q&A to foster engagement during your presentation.

Example: Sarah used PowerPoint Live to present her quarterly report to a global team, enabling participants to follow along at their own pace.

With these tips and tricks, you're ready to take your PowerPoint presentations to the next level.

YOUR AI-POWERED PRESENTATION PARTNER

Imagine having a personal assistant who understands your presentation needs, suggests creative layouts, helps refine your content, and even provides real-time feedback on your delivery. That's the power of Copilot in Microsoft PowerPoint. This AI-driven tool simplifies the creation process, elevates your designs, and enhances the way you deliver presentations.

In this chapter, we'll explore how Copilot transforms PowerPoint into a smarter, more intuitive tool, saving you time and helping you craft impactful presentations.

Copilot is an AI-powered feature integrated into Microsoft PowerPoint, designed to assist users with everything from slide design to content generation. By leveraging advanced machine learning, Copilot analyzes your content and provides intelligent suggestions to enhance your slides.

Key Capabilities Include:

- Generating text and ideas for your slides.
- Recommending layouts and visual enhancements.
- Streamlining complex tasks like creating timelines or designing charts.
- Providing feedback on presentation pacing and tone during rehearsals.

Example: Sarah needed a slide summarizing her company's goals for the year. With a simple prompt to Copilot—"Create a summary of our 2024 goals"—the tool generated concise, well-structured bullet points, complete with design suggestions.

How Copilot Enhances PowerPoint

1. **Design Assistance**

What It Does:
Copilot analyzes your content and suggests professional designs, layouts, and color schemes to make your slides visually appealing.

How It Helps:
- Reduces the time spent on design decisions.
- Ensures a polished, cohesive look for your presentation.

Example: Sarah added a graph to her slide, and Copilot suggested a layout that seamlessly integrated the graph with her key points, enhancing the slide's readability.

Pro Tip: Use Copilot's design suggestions as a starting point, then customize to align with your branding.

2. **Content Generation**

What It Does:
Need help filling a slide? Copilot generates text, bullet points, or even entire slide content based on your input.

How It Helps:
- Saves time by eliminating writer's block.
- Ensures clarity and structure in your message.

Example: Sarah prompted Copilot with "Summarize the benefits of our new product," and it generated concise, audience-focused points that she refined and added to her slide.

Pro Tip: Be specific with your prompts to get results tailored to your needs.

3. **Data Visualization**

What It Does:
Copilot can transform raw data into professional visuals like charts, graphs, and infographics.

How It Helps:
- Makes complex data more digestible.
- Automatically matches visual elements to your presentation's style.

Example: Sarah imported sales data from Excel, and Copilot suggested a bar chart that clearly illustrated trends over time.

Pro Tip: Review and tweak Copilot-generated visuals to ensure they align with your message.

4. AI-Powered Rehearsal Feedback

What It Does:
Copilot evaluates your delivery during practice sessions, offering feedback on pacing, tone, and word choice.

How It Helps:
- Builds confidence by highlighting areas for improvement.
- Helps you refine your delivery for maximum impact.

Example: Sarah used Copilot to rehearse her investor pitch. The tool flagged that she was speaking too quickly on key slides, allowing her to adjust her pacing.

Pro Tip: Practice multiple times with Copilot to track your progress and refine your presentation skills.

Using Copilot Effectively

1. Be Specific with Prompts:
The more detail you provide, the more tailored Copilot's suggestions will

be. For example, instead of "Create a slide about sales," try "Create a slide summarizing Q1 sales performance in a bar chart."

2. Combine AI and Human Insight:
While Copilot can generate great ideas, your personal input ensures the presentation reflects your voice and intent.

3. Explore Its Full Potential:
Experiment with Copilot in different scenarios—whether designing slides, generating ideas, or practicing your delivery—to understand its capabilities.

Copilot isn't just a convenience—it's a powerful ally in creating impactful presentations with less effort. Its ability to automate repetitive tasks, offer creative suggestions, and refine your delivery transforms the way you use PowerPoint.

COMMON PITFALLS AND HOW TO AVOID THEM

Even with a powerful tool like Microsoft PowerPoint, it's easy to fall into traps that can detract from your presentation's impact. From overloading slides with information to underutilizing key features, these missteps can distract your audience and dilute your message. The good news? With a little planning and awareness, you can avoid these common pitfalls and create presentations that are clear, engaging, and professional.

In this chapter, we'll explore frequent PowerPoint mistakes and provide actionable strategies to overcome them.

1. Overloading Slides with Text

The Pitfall:
Slides crammed with text make it difficult for your audience to focus and retain information.

Why It Happens:
Presenters often use slides as a script, including every detail they plan to say.

How to Avoid It:

- Limit text to key points or short bullet lists.
- Use the Notes section for detailed explanations you'll share verbally.
- Emphasize visuals, like charts, images, or icons, to complement your message.

Example: Sarah initially created a slide filled with dense paragraphs explaining her company's mission. By summarizing it into three bullet points and adding a compelling image, she kept her audience engaged.

Pro Tip: Follow the "6x6 Rule": no more than six words per line and six lines per slide.

2. Ignoring Visual Design Principles

The Pitfall:
Poor design choices, such as clashing colors or inconsistent fonts, can distract your audience and undermine your credibility.

Why It Happens:
Presenters may not prioritize design or are unaware of basic principles.

How to Avoid It:

- Stick to a consistent theme or template.
- Choose high-contrast colors for readability.
- Limit fonts to two styles: one for headings and another for body text.

Example: Sarah's first attempt at her presentation included multiple font styles and mismatched colors. After applying a cohesive theme and consistent fonts, her slides looked polished and professional.

Pro Tip: Use PowerPoint's Designer tool for layout and design suggestions that enhance visual appeal.

3. Overusing Animations and Transitions

The Pitfall:
Excessive use of animations or flashy transitions can distract from your content and appear unprofessional.

Why It Happens:
Animations are often added for fun without considering their purpose.

How to Avoid It:

- Use subtle transitions, like Fade or Wipe, to maintain a professional tone.
- Apply animations sparingly to highlight key points or guide the audience's focus.
- Avoid using multiple animation styles in one presentation.

Example: Sarah replaced her spinning and bouncing text animations with a simple fade-in effect, ensuring her content remained the focus.

Pro Tip: Preview your presentation to ensure animations and transitions enhance, rather than distract from, your message.

4. Neglecting Accessibility

The Pitfall:
Slides that aren't accessible exclude audience members with disabilities or impairments.

Why It Happens:
Presenters may not consider accessibility needs during design.

How to Avoid It:
- Use PowerPoint's Accessibility Checker to identify and fix issues.
- Add alt text to images and graphics.
- Ensure sufficient color contrast for text and background elements.

Example: Sarah adjusted her slide colors to improve contrast and added alt text to her images, ensuring her presentation was accessible to all team members.

Pro Tip: Use simple, high-contrast themes and avoid overly complex visuals.

5. Failing to Practice Delivery

The Pitfall:
Even the best slides can fall flat if the presenter isn't confident or prepared.

Why It Happens:
Presenters may focus solely on creating slides and neglect rehearsing their delivery.

How to Avoid It:

- Use PowerPoint's Presenter Coach to practice and receive feedback on your pacing, tone, and use of filler words.
- Time your presentation to ensure you stay within the allotted duration.
- Rehearse in the same environment where you'll present.

Example: Sarah practiced with Presenter Coach, which flagged her tendency to speak too quickly. This helped her adjust her pace for a smooth delivery.

Pro Tip: Record yourself rehearsing to identify areas for improvement.

6. Not Leveraging PowerPoint's Features

The Pitfall:
Underutilizing features like SmartArt, Designer, or Copilot limits the potential of your slides.

Why It Happens:
Presenters may stick to basic tools due to unfamiliarity with advanced features.

How to Avoid It:

- Explore PowerPoint's SmartArt for visually organizing information.
- Use Designer to create professional layouts effortlessly.

- Incorporate Copilot to generate ideas, design slides, and enhance content.

Example: Sarah discovered SmartArt and used it to convert a plain list of objectives into a visually appealing graphic, making her slide more engaging.

Pro Tip: Experiment with features in non-critical presentations to build confidence and proficiency.

7. Forgetting to Tailor Content to the Audience

The Pitfall:
Generic presentations fail to resonate with the specific needs or interests of the audience.

Why It Happens:
Presenters may reuse slides without customizing them for a new audience.

How to Avoid It:

- Research your audience's needs and expectations before creating your slides.
- Adjust language, examples, and visuals to align with your audience's perspective.
- Focus on the "what's in it for them" factor in your content.

Example: Sarah adapted her internal team update slides for a client presentation by adding relevant industry examples, ensuring her audience felt the content was tailored to them.

Pro Tip: Begin your presentation by addressing your audience's specific challenges or goals to capture their attention.

8. Rushing the Ending

The Pitfall:
A weak or abrupt conclusion leaves the audience without a clear takeaway or call to action.

Why It Happens:
Presenters may run out of time or fail to plan their closing.

How to Avoid It:

- End with a slide summarizing key points.
- Include a clear call to action or next steps.
- Rehearse your timing to ensure you don't rush through the final slides.

Example: Sarah concluded her pitch with a slide reading, "Join Us in Transforming the Future," paired with a strong visual and clear instructions for next steps.

Pro Tip: Practice your conclusion to ensure it leaves a lasting impression.

By avoiding these common pitfalls, you'll ensure your PowerPoint presentations are clear, professional, and impactful.

SARAH'S POWERPOINT TRANSFORMATION

The sound of fingers typing filled the small office as Sarah sat at her desk, staring at a blank PowerPoint slide. Her team had tasked her with creating the presentation for their upcoming product launch, and she felt the weight of the responsibility. This wasn't just another routine meeting; this presentation would set the tone for the company's future.

"Make it engaging," her manager had said. "We want to wow the investors."

Sarah exhaled sharply. "No pressure," she muttered, opening a template and starting with the title slide.

Sarah's initial slides were cluttered and uninspired. She piled text onto each one, thinking more information would impress the audience. As she worked, the slides felt increasingly chaotic, a reflection of her growing frustration.

"This isn't working," Sarah admitted, closing her laptop for the night.

The next morning, during a quick coffee break, Sarah overheard her colleague James discussing PowerPoint's Designer feature. Intrigued, she decided to give it a try.

Back at her desk, she added a product image to one of her slides. Within seconds, Designer suggested layouts that transformed her slide from bland to eye-catching. "Where has this been all my life?" Sarah thought, her enthusiasm renewed.

She continued experimenting, finding ways to streamline her presentation:

- **SmartArt** helped her turn dense lists into visually appealing graphics.
- **Morph transitions** made her slides flow seamlessly.

- **Presenter View** allowed her to add speaker notes, keeping her on track without overwhelming her slides with text.

One of Sarah's biggest challenges was presenting sales data in a way that didn't bore her audience. Previously, she had relied on spreadsheets copied into slides. Now, she used PowerPoint's charting tools to create clear, colorful visuals.

She transformed raw numbers into bar graphs and pie charts, using animations to reveal trends step by step. "This makes so much more sense," she thought, marveling at how easily her data came to life.

With the bulk of her slides complete, Sarah decided to test out Copilot. She prompted it to "generate a summary of the product's key features," and Copilot delivered a concise, well-structured slide in seconds.

Encouraged, she tried more:

- "Suggest design ideas for the marketing slide."
- "Create an agenda slide for the presentation."
- "Rewrite this bullet list in a more engaging tone."

Copilot even helped her rehearse by analyzing her pacing and flagging areas where she needed to slow down. "It's like having a coach," Sarah mused, feeling more confident with each practice session.

Sarah knew her audience would include investors with varying levels of technical knowledge, so she focused on storytelling. She used animations sparingly to highlight key points and embedded a short video demo of the product to keep them engaged.

For the Q&A session, she prepared an interactive slide with clickable links to supporting materials. PowerPoint Live, integrated with Teams, allowed her audience to explore the slides on their own devices during the presentation.

When the day of the presentation arrived, Sarah stood at the front of the conference room, her laptop connected to the projector. As she clicked through her slides, she noticed the investors leaning forward, nodding in agreement.

The polished design, clear visuals, and engaging delivery kept their attention. By the time she reached the final slide—a bold call to action accompanied by an inspiring product image—Sarah knew she had succeeded.

After the meeting, Sarah's manager approached her with a smile. "That was incredible," he said. "You made it look effortless."

Sarah felt a wave of pride. She had gone from overwhelmed to empowered, mastering tools and techniques that made her message shine.

Sarah's journey highlights the transformative power of PowerPoint. Whether you're a beginner or an experienced user, following best practices and exploring PowerPoint's advanced features can elevate your presentations to new heights.

LESSONS FROM POWERPOINT AND SARAH'S JOURNEY

As we conclude this journey through Microsoft PowerPoint, it's clear that this tool is far more than just software—it's a platform for creativity, communication, and connection. Along the way, we've explored its features, uncovered best practices, and followed Sarah's inspiring story as she transformed her presentation skills and boosted her confidence.

This chapter revisits the key takeaways from the book while reflecting on Sarah's journey and how it mirrors your own path as a learner and presenter.

1. **What Is PowerPoint?**
   PowerPoint is a versatile tool for crafting presentations that inform, persuade, and captivate. Its integration with Microsoft 365 and user-friendly design makes it an essential resource for professionals, educators, and anyone needing to share ideas visually.

2. **Why Use PowerPoint?**
   With PowerPoint, you can simplify complex information, engage your audience with dynamic visuals, and seamlessly integrate with other tools like Teams and SharePoint. It's a trusted ally in presentations of all sizes and purposes.

3. **Getting Started with PowerPoint:**
   From choosing templates to organizing slides, PowerPoint's intuitive interface ensures a smooth start for beginners and flexibility for advanced users.

4. **Best Practices and Tips:**
   Designing with visual hierarchy, using SmartArt and animations sparingly, and practicing with tools like Presenter Coach elevate your presentation from functional to exceptional.

5. **Leveraging Copilot:**
   Copilot enhances productivity with AI-driven suggestions for slide design, content generation, and rehearsal feedback, making PowerPoint smarter and more efficient.

6. **Common Pitfalls:**
   Avoiding cluttered slides, poor design choices, and lack of practice ensures your presentations remain clear, engaging, and professional.

7. **Sarah's Journey:**
   Through Sarah's story, we saw how PowerPoint transformed a daunting task into a rewarding experience, empowering her to create a presentation that resonated with her audience.

Sarah's experience is a testament to the power of learning and growth. She began her journey overwhelmed and unsure, much like many first-time PowerPoint users. But by exploring the tool's features and following best practices, she found her stride and delivered a presentation that exceeded expectations.

Her story mirrors the path you're taking as a reader:

- **Starting Simple:** Like Sarah, you might begin with basic slides, focusing on getting your message across.

- **Exploring Features:** Sarah's discovery of Designer, SmartArt, and Copilot helped her streamline her process and elevate her slides. Similarly, experimenting with PowerPoint's tools can unlock new possibilities for your presentations.

- **Embracing Growth:** Sarah's confidence grew with each step, from organizing her slides to rehearsing her delivery. Your own journey will likely follow a similar trajectory as you apply what you've learned and refine your skills.

The lessons in this book are a foundation for your continued growth with PowerPoint. Each presentation you create is an opportunity to hone your skills, engage your audience, and make an impact.

PowerPoint isn't just about slides; it's about telling stories, sharing ideas, and fostering connections. By leveraging its features and staying mindful of best practices, you can craft presentations that resonate and inspire.

As Sarah's journey reminds us, learning is an ongoing process. The knowledge and confidence you've gained here are just the beginning. PowerPoint is part of the broader Microsoft 365 ecosystem, and exploring its integration with tools like Teams, SharePoint, and OneDrive can unlock even greater potential.

POWERPOINT AND BEYOND

As we reach the end of this book, it's worth stepping back to see the bigger picture of what Microsoft PowerPoint represents. It's more than just software for creating slides; it's a tool that amplifies your voice, organizes your thoughts, and connects you with your audience.

PowerPoint has stood the test of time because it evolves alongside the changing needs of its users. From its intuitive design features to its seamless integration with Microsoft 365 and innovative additions like Copilot, PowerPoint continues to empower individuals and teams to communicate effectively and creatively.

At its heart, PowerPoint is about storytelling—taking complex ideas and presenting them in a way that's clear, engaging, and memorable. Whether you're explaining data trends, sharing a vision, or pitching a groundbreaking idea, PowerPoint gives you the tools to make your story resonate.

Sarah's journey throughout this book reflects the transformative potential of PowerPoint. She began as a hesitant presenter but grew into a confident communicator, using the features and strategies outlined here. Her experience mirrors the journey many of us take when we step outside our comfort zones to grow and learn.

Your journey doesn't stop here. Like Sarah, you've taken the first steps to mastering PowerPoint, but there's always room for growth. Each presentation you create is an opportunity to refine your skills and push the boundaries of what's possible.

One of PowerPoint's greatest strengths is its ability to work seamlessly with other Microsoft 365 tools. As you continue exploring PowerPoint, consider how it integrates with the larger ecosystem:

- **Microsoft Teams:** Present directly within Teams meetings, making collaboration effortless.

- **SharePoint and OneDrive:** Store and share presentations securely in the cloud, ensuring accessibility from any device.
- **Excel:** Bring data to life with charts and graphs that dynamically update with changes in Excel.
- **Copilot:** Use AI-driven insights across multiple tools to streamline your workflow and elevate your output.

Each tool enhances PowerPoint's capabilities, creating a cohesive, powerful suite of resources that amplifies productivity and creativity.

Technology is always evolving, and staying ahead requires a commitment to continuous learning. PowerPoint will continue to introduce new features and integrations, offering more ways to create and connect. By embracing these changes and seeking out new resources, you can remain at the forefront of effective communication.

This book is part of the *Microsoft 365 Companion Series*, a collection of guides designed to help you unlock the potential of the tools you use every day. Whether it's PowerPoint, Teams, OneDrive, or any other Microsoft 365 app, there's always more to discover. Each book in this series offers unique insights and practical advice to help you grow.

Take what you've learned in this book and apply it. Start with your next presentation, and challenge yourself to use a new feature, try a new design technique, or integrate PowerPoint with another tool in the Microsoft 365 suite.

The path to mastery is built one step at a time, and every improvement, no matter how small, brings you closer to becoming a confident, effective communicator.

Thank you for taking this journey through PowerPoint. The skills you've gained here are tools for transformation—not just in how you create presentations, but in how you share your ideas and connect with others.

As you continue to grow, remember that PowerPoint is just one piece of the puzzle. The Microsoft 365 ecosystem offers a world of possibilities to enhance your productivity and creativity. Explore it, embrace it, and keep learning.

Here's to your success with PowerPoint and beyond!

www.ingramcontent.com/pod-product-compliance
Lightning Source LLC
Chambersburg PA
CBHW070940220526
45469CB00007B/2458